Secrets to Goal Setting Success

A FeelFabToday Guide
By Rachel Robins

Secrets To
Goal Setting Success

All rights reserved.

This publication is copyright protected and is intended for personal use only. No part of this publication may be altered or reproduced in any form or by any means, electronic, mechanical, photocopying, recording or otherwise transmitted without express written permission from the author.

This book is for informational purposes only and no parts should be considered as medical advice. You must not rely on the information in this publication as a substitute to advice from a medical professional such as your doctor or other professional heath care provider.

This book is for informational purposes only, and no warranties of any kind are expressed or implied. Although every precaution has been taken in the preparation of this work, neither the author, publisher, affiliates or partners shall have any liability to any person or entity with respect to any loss or damage caused or alleged to be caused directly or indirectly by the information contained in this book. Readers acknowledge that the author is not offering legal, financial, medical or professional advice.

Copyright © 2014 Rachel Robins

Cover and internal vector images credited to:
© trueffelpix /Fotolia

ISBN-13: 978-1499714623
ISBN-10: 1499714629

Table of Contents

1/What to Expect From This Book	5
2/What Goal Setting Is All About	11
Are They Really Yours?	13
What Types Of Goals Can You Set?	15
What Methods Should You Use?	20
Reality And Expectations	24
Is It A Goal Or A Task?	27
What Is An Effective Goal?	31
What Issues Are Holding You Back?	32
3/ Why Bother Setting Goals	35
Why Goals Are So Powerful	37
Identify Why A Goal Is Important To *You*	39
Take Control	40
Being A Better You	42
4/ How To Be A Successful Goal Achiever	45
Tip 1 - Know Where You Are Today	46
Tip 2-3 - Re-train Your Brain	47
Tip 4 - Understand Where You Are Headed	52
Tip 5-6 - Commitment And Motivation	53

Tip 7 - Prioritize And Choose Your Goals Carefully	57
Tip 8-13 - Select Your Methods And Tools	61
Tip 14 - Effective Execution	74
Tip 15 - Get Organized	77
Tip 16 - Fight Fear And Doubt	80
Tip 17 - Eliminate Distractions And Obstacles	83
Tip 18 - New Helpful Habits	88
Tip 19 - Maintain Forward Momentum	91
Tip 20 - Stop And Review	94
Tip 21-22 - Milestones And Rewards	98
Worksheets And Resources	103
Exercises And Action Points	112
5/ Final Thoughts	124
6/ Next Steps	128
7/ About The Author	134
8/ And Finally	136

1

What to Expect From This Book

*"If you focus on results, you will never change.
If you focus on change, you will get results."
~ Jack Dixon*

This book is all about goal setting, and how to easily fulfill those goals, so you always, always get what you want.

However, you've no doubt heard it all before – 'you <u>must</u> set goals', 'goals are hard work', 'you won't achieve anything without a goal', and so on. These sort of statements make goal setting sound like hard work, and something to be avoided.

The reality is, goal setting can be *simple, fun* and *empowering.* Goal achievement then becomes so much simpler.

Most of us have become stuck at one point or other. Our plans may have become confused or inconsistent. Perhaps we've followed the lead from our peers, or tried to meet family expectations, when, in truth, these actions were not in line with our own true desires.

Sometimes, we hold back from attempting a new project because we worry about our lack of ability, confidence, or experience. Or, maybe our circumstances, the influence of others and our own self belief holds us back.

The good news is none of these issues need prevent us from setting and accomplishing both small and large goals. Throughout this book, we'll explore numerous ways as to how you can choose the *right* goals, create *effective* plans, take action, and achieve awesome results.

If you've struggled to achieve your goals in the past, there's a reason:

WHAT TO EXPECT FROM THIS BOOK

- Desire is not strong enough
- Lacking real motivation
- Time constraints
- Poor organizational skills
- Goal wasn't realistic
- Procrastination issues
- Problems focusing

Any of those sound familiar? How often have you settled on a course of action, but then just didn't follow through with it? Unfortunately, this is the norm for most people. It's not because we're lazy, lack self discipline, or are incapable of completing the project. It's because we didn't have the right motivation to achieve the goal in the first place, it was never realistic, or we weren't using an effective method to give us the results we hoped for.

Goals can be hard to achieve for a number of reasons. They require an understanding of *why* you want the outcome, what steps you need to take, a set of tools to support you, and a strong desire to achieve them. If it was always easy, everyone would be exactly where they wanted to be. The reality is that goal setting, and achievement, can be hard work, frustrating, and easy to get wrong. Many people give up half way through, or fall at the first hurdle without getting up. **Don't be that person**.

SECRETS TO GOAL SETTING SUCCESS

"I've failed over and over and over again in my life. And that is why I succeed."
~ Michael Jordan

This book is not about asking you to change your personality to suit certain methods, nor does it try to reinvent the wheel. There are many different styles of goal setting; some are complex and time-consuming, others are simple and easy to implement. We aim to demonstrate that achieving your goals can be made simple, when you focus on the right things, and do them well.

In chapter 2, you'll discover **what** goal setting is all about. We take a good look at the various methods you can use, the types of goals you can set, and whether you are managing your own expectations correctly.

Chapter 3 reveals **why** goals are so powerful. We discuss why it's absolutely vital to understand their importance to *you*, and why you should bother to set them in the first place.

Then, in chapter 4, we explore **how** you can get the results you want. We identify a variety of methods and tools you can use; we look at how to manage fears, distractions, and commitment issues, and how to create an effective plan of attack.

We've also included plenty of realistic examples, with easy to follow methods and techniques that everyone can easily apply. There are seven action-oriented exercises you can carry out to stretch your thought muscles, and help you focus on your fabulous new plans. Plus, there are goal setting worksheets you can link to for personal use.

> *"A mind that has been stretched will never return to its original dimension."*
> ~ *Albert Einstein*

Throughout the book we delve into the details relating to various methods, and the many steps you can take. However, *you* are ultimately the best judge for what works for you. Be selective. Be self critical where necessary, but also be supportive toward yourself. Know that you *can* discover a system that works well for you, and that with the right set of actions, you *will* achieve the results you desire.

When you apply the tips and techniques in this book, you'll have made a huge step toward creating your ideal future. You'll be empowered to:

- Quickly identify limiting beliefs
- Uncover the root causes as to why you're stuck
- Eliminate barriers that hold you back
- Conquer your goal setting fears and self-doubt
- Overpower obstacles, and wipe out distractions
- Identify small and large goals that matter most

- Assemble a set of super-supportive tools
- Design effective solutions that work, time and time again
- Develop helpful habits to support your goals
- Amaze your friends and family with your new found attitude
- Create lasting change and improve the quality of your life

We hope you'll be inspired to look at goal setting and goal achievement with a fresh approach, that you'll find confidence in yourself, to unquestioningly believe you can accomplish more in your life, in much less time than you originally thought possible. When you start to experience fast, effective results, you'll feel motivated to achieve more and more. Observing how your own actions can create your desired outcomes is both exciting and empowering. You'll then unreservedly believe in your own ability to create a happy, healthy and fulfilling future.

Let this be your guide, so you can uncover the secrets to your own goal setting success.

1

What Goal Setting Is All About

Defining what goals really mean to *you* is an important step in turning them into a reality.

By setting goals for yourself, you're making positive choices about your future. When you understand what motivates you, and can clearly define what you want to accomplish, you can focus your efforts in the best way possible. You'll be able to easily remove obstacles or distractions, and reach your desired outcome in a much faster time frame.

SECRETS TO GOAL SETTING SUCCESS

Setting realistic goals, and taking meaningful steps to achieve them, is a powerful way to control your life.

Discovering efficient and effective techniques for goal setting, along with establishing meaningful activities, means you'll be more likely to see a successful outcome. Plus, you'll reach your desired outcome in a much swifter way, than if you meander without direction.

Merriam-Webster dictionary definitions:

Efficient - capable of producing desired results without wasting materials, time, or energy

Effective - producing a result that is wanted: having an intended effect

---

"There is nothing so useless as doing efficiently that which should not be done at all."
~ Peter Drucker

Throughout this book, we'll explore steps that are both *efficient* and *effective*, to help you effortlessly deliver the results you desire.

WHAT GOAL SETTING IS ALL ABOUT

Are They Really Yours?

When you think about your current or future goals, do they really *feel* like yours (or something you're being asked to do for someone else)?

It's critical for you to completely own your goals, so you can achieve them in a manner that's easy and enjoyable.

Any goals you're going to actively work on need to be yours, and no one else's. Although shared goals can be great, the goal must also be truly yours. It's important to be able to work at your own pace, and to define your own version of what success looks like.

"Motivation is a fire from within.
If someone else tries to light that fire under you,
chances are it will burn very briefly."
~ Stephen R. Covey

Unfortunately, expectations from other people can sometimes have a powerful influence over us. We, therefore, need to be careful not to allow them to steer us in a direction we don't want to go, without exerting our own influence on what choices we make.

SECRETS TO GOAL SETTING SUCCESS

Examples of other people's expectations:

- Your family expects you to settle down and start your own family **versus** you want to travel the world, swim with dolphins in the ocean, and conquer difficult mountains, before you think about starting a family.
- Your parents expect you to follow the family tradition and become a doctor / lawyer / optician / join the military **versus** you want to be an actor on Broadway.
- Your spouse wants you to stay at home and raise the children **versus** you want to work as well
- Your boss wants you to apply for promotion **versus** you don't want the added responsibility, and aren't interested in the type of tasks you'd need to take on.

If we're expected to work toward something we're not passionate about, we're not likely to do our best. Or, even if you strive to achieve the expected outcome, the result is unlikely to make you truly happy. However, working on *your* goals, or a mutually agreed compromise, will be so much more satisfying.

WHAT GOAL SETTING IS ALL ABOUT

"Always bear in mind that your own resolution to succeed is more important than any other"
~ Abraham Lincoln

Having said that, shared goals, which align to your true desires, can be incredibly powerful. When you work toward a shared goal with a friend, colleague, spouse, or child, you'll find oodles of encouragement and inspiration that wouldn't be possible without their involvement.

What Types Of Goals Can You Set?

There are all sorts of goals you can set, and each type may be appropriate at different stages of your life.

For example, you can set:

- **Big,** long-term, challenging goals that will stretch your capabilities.
- **Small,** manageable goals, that allow you to consistently achieve (and could be tied into a larger set of goals)

Large goals need to be mapped out carefully, and broken into manageable chunks. With the smaller stages

SECRETS TO GOAL SETTING SUCCESS

identified, you'll be able to clearly see your progression toward the end game.

Goals can also be given labels such as *personal, shared, S.M.A.R.T., visualized, objective* or *performance based* and so on.

Choosing the *right* type of goals to work on is essential. They will reflect your personal style and preference, and, therefore, enable you to efficiently plan and effectively carry them out, in accordance with the approach they require.

Goals can also be broken down into categories, which enable you to specifically focus on the areas of your life that are most important to you.

WHAT GOAL SETTING IS ALL ABOUT

Areas you can build goals around include:

Job, Career or Business
- Find a new job or opportunity
- Work toward a promotion
- Start or expand a business
- Develop new skills or gain qualifications
- Create an online business for weekends/evenings
- Better use of your personal strengths

Health and Wellness
- Manage stress
- Healthy eating and energizing
- Exercise and fitness activities
- Pain or illness management
- Quality of sleep
- Motivation and happiness

Self Improvement
- Build new, powerful habits
- Education and developing new skills
- Overcome fear or doubt
- Time management skills
- Eliminate procrastination
- Build confidence and self esteem
- Develop a positive mindset
- Feeling and looking great

SECRETS TO GOAL SETTING SUCCESS

Family and Friends
- Spend quality time with loved ones
- Actively listen and pay attention
- Enjoy shared activities
- Show them how much they mean to you
- Support and encourage their goals and dreams
- Be a great parent/child/friend/spouse

Personal Relationships
- Strengthen important relationships
- Remove or reduce time-wasters and toxic relationships
- Seek new relationships with supportive, motivating people
- Improve communication skills
- Identify personal behaviors that hold you back, and find solutions

Home
- Create a happy, welcoming home
- De-clutter and become organized
- Cleaning projects
- Re-decoration or improvements
- Create a new theme

Finances and Money Management
- Create budgets, saving, and investments
- Mortgage and debt management

WHAT GOAL SETTING IS ALL ABOUT

- Personal finance overhaul
- Insurance protection
- Pension planning
- Financial advice and guidance

Fun
- Travel and vacation planning
- Hobbies/artistic expression – paint, write, sing!
- Sports and adrenaline fueled activities
- Self care and *me* time
- Things that make you happy
- Family activities

Vocational
- Volunteer for a good cause
- Be a good neighbor.
- Become active in your community
- Seek activities that reflect your values
- Work as part of a team for a cause that's close to your heart

Spiritual and Religious
- Join a like-minded group/s
- Participate in local activities
- Strengthen your faith
- Seek guidance and support
- Offer your services

Once you are completely clear on which goals you want to focus on, you can prioritize the ones that matter most, and choose the best techniques to fulfill them.

Which ever ones you pick, they should inspire you, excite you, and create in you a fierce determination to succeed.

What Methods Should You Use?

> *"Talk does not cook rice"*
> *~- Chinese Proverb*

When you talk about something you want, you're making a statement. That's not the same as setting, and accomplishing, a goal.

Talk without action, means nothing moves forward.

However, turning words into action can be easier said than done. Fortunately, when you identify a method

WHAT GOAL SETTING IS ALL ABOUT

of goal setting you are comfortable with, and inspired by, you'll find it far easier to stick to.

Assuming you've chosen goals you're passionate about, you'll need to follow processes that resonate well with *you*. When you follow steps that work well for you, it means you're much more likely to maintain focus, and keep the momentum going.

There are many methods you can use, such as:

- Create visual prompts, for example picture boards, Post-its, motivational quotes, etc, to keep you focused on your target goals.
- Write your goals down, and place them prominently, where you'll see them every day.
- Record your journey in a diary or journal, for daily motivation, and subconscious reiteration.
- State your goals out load, list the benefits, and commit to them frequently.
- Share them with people you trust, and who will support and encourage you. Make yourself accountable.
- Visualize the successful outcome, and keep that image front of your mind.

SECRETS TO GOAL SETTING SUCCESS

- Use the S.M.A.R.T steps to be specific, measurable, achievable, realistic and time-bound.
- Use daily to-do lists to ensure consistent steps are taken.
- Set your goals into an app on your smart phone or tablet, so they're with you wherever you go.

Using strategy and tactics

You can use a specific strategy, combined with individual tactics, to efficiently plan and execute your goals.

In terms of goal setting, this means you'll have an overall strategy to get where you need to go, plus, you'll identify individual tactical steps to consistently move you forward.

Merriam-Webster dictionary definitions:

Strategy - a careful plan or method for achieving a particular goal usually over a long period of time

Tactic - an action or method that is planned and used to achieve a particular goal

---

WHAT GOAL SETTING IS ALL ABOUT

For example, you want to learn 50 new recipes.

Your strategy is: to learn, then practice, one new recipe a week, for the next 50 weeks.

Your tactics are:

- Create a list of specific recipes
- Visit your friend who's a great cook, once a week to work alongside her
- Practice the recipes at home by yourself, later in the week
- Repeat the recipe at least twice during the next four weeks, or until you're happy with the results.
- Celebrate after the 50th recipe by taking your friend out to the theatre

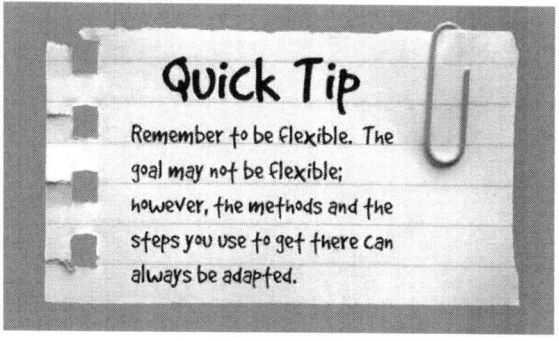

Quick Tip

Remember to be flexible. The goal may not be flexible; however, the methods and the steps you use to get there can always be adapted.

SECRETS TO GOAL SETTING SUCCESS

*"Map out your future,
but do it in pencil"*
~ *Jon Bon Jovi*

We often need to re-prioritize, as life changes. Keep in mind that the goal (or the outcome) should continue to excite and inspire you. If something in your life changes or you no longer feel motivated to accomplish the goal, then it's time to reassess where you're going, and change course, if necessary.

Reality And Expectations

Having goals is easy.
Setting them is more complicated.
Achieving them is more complicated still.

As we discussed at the start of the book, there are many reasons why we don't succeed in reaching our goals. It's possibly because:

- They're too complicated
- Unrealistic
- Not enough time
- Lack of commitment
- Not really your goal, but someone else's
- Obstacles or distractions

WHAT GOAL SETTING IS ALL ABOUT

- Procrastination
- Poor organizational skills
- Haphazard method

One thing is for certain – we don't have enough time to achieve everything we'd like, as quickly as we'd like. Biting off more than you can chew, running round like a headless chicken, becoming disheartened and abandoning projects, these are all issues which people regularly face, and can prevent them from succeeding.

However, by choosing goals that we are motivated by, prioritizing them, and using effective methods to steer us, then we can be miles ahead of the game.

If your goal setting has not worked for you in the past, then it may be time to take a reality check.

Have you suffered from any of the issues in the above list?

Let's look at an exercising goal as an example:

People set exercise goals for many reasons – to get fit, tackle a debilitating health issue, build muscle definition, improve life expectancy, train for a specific event, new sporting opportunity or social interaction, overall enjoyment, and so on.

SECRETS TO GOAL SETTING SUCCESS

It's important to understand exactly *why* you're setting an exercise goal, so you can be realistic about what outcome will make you happy, and what you can reasonably expect to gain from the process.

Ask yourself what specific outcome you want?

- Better body appearance
- Able to run after the children and play games with them
- Improve sleep patterns
- Manage pain or stress issues
- Run a marathon for charity
- Meet new people
- Participate in a competitive sport
- Improve overall heath and wellness

Once you have a clear idea *what exactly* you'd like to gain from the process, you'll be able to take the right steps toward the end goal.

Without this understanding you could end up frustrated and disappointed. Imagine you set a goal to get fit. You join the local gym with a friend, and attend after work sessions twice a week for two months. You start to notice the difference during your cardiovascular workouts, and your muscle tone is building up nicely.

However, you still feel stressed out, and are not sleeping well at night.

If your underlying desire was to manage your stress levels, to feel less tired, and to feel better in yourself, then this exercise routine was not best suited to the reality of your goal. You would be more likely to achieve your desired outcome with a morning exercise workout, plus some relaxation based classes, e.g. yoga or Pilates, and an improved diet.

When you align your activities to the genuine, stripped back reasons for your goal, you'll achieve your desired result much faster. Be realistic about the outcome of any activities you undertake, and you'll easily manage your own expectations.

Then, with well directed activities, you'll achieve the outcome you wanted, feel immensely satisfied and proud of yourself, and motivated to set new goals.

Be honest with yourself; be crystal clear on your reasons. The steps to achieving your ideal outcome will then naturally follow. Correctly manage your own expectations, and you'll get yourself to a confident and happy place.

Is It A Goal Or A Task?

Goals and tasks are closely related, and are often confused.

SECRETS TO GOAL SETTING SUCCESS

The goal is the overall objective, i.e., your desired outcome.

The tasks are the individual actions required to get you closer to the outcome.

> **Merriam-Webster dictionary definitions:**
>
> ***Goal*** — something that you are trying to do or achieve
>
> ***Task*** — a piece of work that has been given to someone: a job for someone to do (often to be finished within a certain time).

The line can, however, become blurry, especially on larger projects. Each task is a step toward the main goal. However, it can also be treated as a mini goal in itself.

It may be easier, therefore, to define a goal as an objective, an aim, or a dream. Your ultimate objective will then be achieved by dividing it into manageable tasks, steps, or action points.

Having a clear goal in mind steers us in the right direction, and helps focus us sharply on the end result. Unfortunately though, the required tasks can sometimes be too complicated, overwhelming, or be missed/forgotten. If we do veer off track, stopping to

WHAT GOAL SETTING IS ALL ABOUT

review the main goal can snap us back into focus, and re-energize us toward taking the right actions.

As an example, you set a goal to make an amazing cheese soufflé.

The tasks involved could be:

- Find an easy recipe to start with.
- Conduct research on the Internet for tips on successful soufflé making.
- Buy the ingredients.
- Practice on a day when you have time (and don't have guests waiting for dinner!).
- Keep practicing until you have the perfect, mouthwatering, cheese soufflé.
- Invite guests to dinner and share your masterpiece. Bask in the glory!

Each of the above steps could also be seen as a mini goal. For example, you set yourself a goal to visit the local library and borrow three cookbooks with soufflé recipes, so you can study them in the evening. To ensure that really happens, you may need to break that goal down further:

- Set aside at least 20 minutes at lunch to pop into the library.
- Remember to take your library card with you.
- Take a bag to carry the books around later.
- Set aside time that evening, after the kids have gone to bed, to study the books.
- Make a side note to create a list of potential ingredients, ready for the supermarket run later in the week.

As you can see, goals and tasks can be inter-related. However, having a clear goal, or objective, to start with, will influence and guide you as to the individual tasks, or steps you need to take.

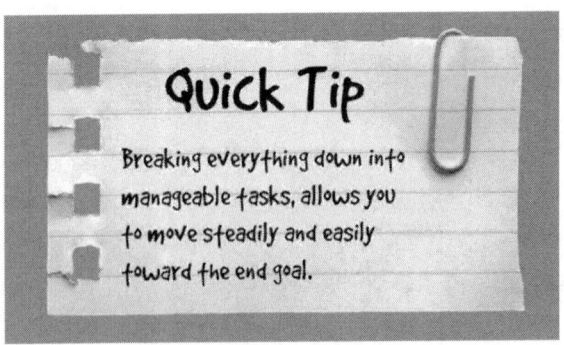

Quick Tip

Breaking everything down into manageable tasks, allows you to move steadily and easily toward the end goal.

"It is not enough to take steps which may some day lead to a goal;

WHAT GOAL SETTING IS ALL ABOUT

*each step must be itself a goal
and a step likewise."*
~ *Johann Wolfgang von Goethe*

What Is An Effective Goal?

Referring back to the definition we looked at earlier,

'**Effective** = producing a result that is wanted: having an intended effect'.

There is a huge difference between thinking about a goal, and actually setting it in such a way that you effortlessly achieve the outcome you desire. Unfortunately, many of us have goals we'd really like to achieve, yet we become stuck somewhere along the way.

Most of the reasons we fail to realize our goals are listed in the previous section on *Reality and Expectations*. For example, the goals were:

- Too complex or unrealistic.
- We didn't allow enough time to work on them, or gave up too soon.
- We weren't motivated enough to see them through.
- We became distracted, or allowed an obstacle to prevent us from progressing.

- We didn't have a robust system in place.
- We weren't really clear on the end goal.
- We let fear or doubt hold us back.

"I don't care how much power, brilliance or energy you have, if you don't harness it and focus it on a specific target, and hold it there you're never going to accomplish as much as your ability warrants."
~ Zig Ziglar

There are various highly effective methods we can put in place, to enable an effective outcome. Later on, in the section on *'How to Achieve'*, we'll explore a range of simple steps you can take, to guarantee great results.

Goals that are not aligned with our true motivations, or are simply unrealistic, are unlikely to provide a successful outcome. Whereas, when we set goals that make our heart race, and divide them into manageable tasks, we'll quickly see positive results, and be able to celebrate our amazing accomplishments.

What Issues Are Holding You Back?

Having goals inside your head, but never seeming to realize them, can be extremely frustrating. There are a number of issues that are primarily responsible for holding us back, making us feel stuck, or providing disappointing results.

If we can address these, and remove the blockages, we can freely move forward.

Do you recognize any of the following?

- Fear of failure
- Lack of support
- Poor advice
- Family expectations
- Bad circumstances
- Other priorities
- Poor health
- Feeling overwhelmed
- Disappointing previous results
- Easily being distracted
- Lack of confidence
- Self sabotage

Identify the issues that are personal to you, and you can find solutions to move past them.

It's perfectly normal to find yourself suffering from fear, questioning your ability, procrastinating or feeling overwhelmed by the prospect of taking action. It's also a common problem to become distracted by time-wasting activities, or people who drain your energy.

The good news is that solutions can be found to remove all of these issues. Recognizing them is the first step. Committing to get past them is the second. **Focus on a small, but clear goal to start with.** Find one that truly motivates you, and go for it, regardless of obstacles or fears.

The very fact that you accomplish something you wanted, and fast, will demonstrate that you *can* do it. Then, take on something bigger!

3

Why Bother Setting Goals

Successful people in all walks of life, including sports persons, entrepreneurs, and senior business managers recognize the importance of setting goals, and the huge benefts they can derive from setting clearly defined targets. They consistently use clever and effective goal techniques to their personal and professional advantage.

SECRETS TO GOAL SETTING SUCCESS

Strongly defined goals allow you to have a reference point to aim for, and sharply bring into focus the outcomes you desire. The sense of achievement and pride you experience on attainment of the goal is as much a benefit as the specific enjoyment the outcome then brings you.

> *"Setting goals is the first step in turning the invisible into the visible."*
> *~ Anthony Robbins*

Furthermore, each time you prove you can succeed at something that initially seemed out of reach, you're spurred on to tackle the next set of stretching goals.

We all have goals in our life anyway, even in a minor, unrecognized way. We may have the goal of getting out of bed on time every day, remembering to eat healthy snacks instead of calorie-laden chocolate bars, finding a new car, or returning books to the library to avoid a fine. These may not be life altering tasks, but nevertheless, we still set them as an objective, and need to work to achieve them.

Effective, forward-thinking goal setting means we're focused on a specific target that will bring positive benefits. Large or small, all meaningful goals are worthy of effective execution.

Why Goals Are So Powerful

*"People with goals succeed because
they know where they're going."*
~ Earl Nightingale

A well defined, motivating goal, with distinct action points, can be powerful in so many ways. Great goals can push you out of a rut, help you achieve loads more in less time, stop you running around like a headless chicken, and give you more time to spend on things you love doing.

Powerful goals can:

- Allow you to focus on what matters most
- Let you take control of your life
- Push you to achieve so much more than you imagined was possible
- Improve creativity and make you more solution oriented
- Build confidence and boost self esteem
- Develop new abilities and then strengthen your capabilities
- Motivate you to take on more
- Make you feel good about yourself

SECRETS TO GOAL SETTING SUCCESS

- Eliminate excuses
- Deliver your ideal future, faster than expected
- Make you happy

Successfully achieving any project we set for ourselves, and being able to enjoy the fruits of our labor is a fantastic thing. We are able to feel an intense sense of satisfaction, empowerment, pride, and a ton of other positive emotions.

Plus, if we've had to overcome obstacles along the way, manage our fears, tackle disappointments or remove distractions, then we're also building a higher level of resilience to life's problems. We prove to ourselves that we can accomplish some amazing results, despite the speed bumps we encounter. Our self belief improves, along with our appetite to take on more and more challenges.

"Success isn't a result of spontaneous combustion.
You must set yourself on fire."
~ Arnold H. Glasow

As you begin to benefit from more success in your life, and develop new sets of skills, along with seeing the profits from your actions, then your happiness levels will increase. And being happy is a great place to be!

Identify Why A Goal Is Important To *You*

When you've established a set of goals, identify *why* you want to achieve them.

For example:

- Feel better in body or mind
- Become unstuck, move forward
- Get more done, in less time
- Make a contribution to others
- Prove something to yourself or others
- Express your values or beliefs
- Enjoyment of the process
- Simply to benefit from the outcome

Your personal why is a powerful thing. It can tie in to a sense of purpose, and can be the element that sparks your passion.

There will be some significant motivating factor as to why you want to achieve your specific goals. Do something positive with that desire, and find a way to guarantee a great result.

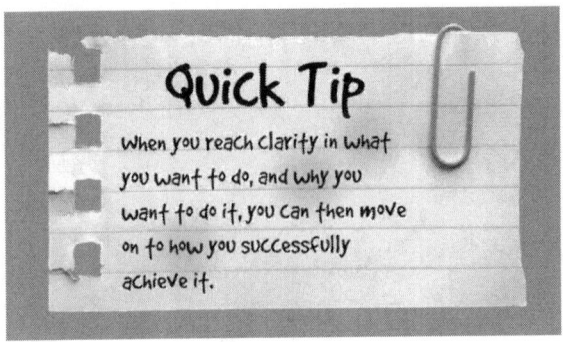

Quick Tip: When you reach clarity in what you want to do, and why you want to do it, you can then move on to how you successfully achieve it.

Take Control

Being in control of your life means you can actively shape your future.

Goal setting is a powerful way to take charge of where you're going and what you're doing. It allows you to actively decide who you spend your time with, and what activities you become involved in. When you have a specific set of tasks to achieve each day, designed to move you closer to your goals, you'll be extra motivated to achieve them.

Taking control means eliminating time-wasting people and activities. When you find yourself chatting to someone who's rambling on about unimportant stuff, you'll be mindful to cut the conversation short, so you can focus on a productive task on your list instead.

There are many insignificant ways in which time can slip by. During that time, you could have completed something on your task list, taking you one step closer to your goal.

WHY BOTHER SETTING GOALS

Recognize any of these?

- Watching a silly TV program
- Reading a gossip magazine
- Playing with your mobile phone
- Looking at Facebook, Twitter, or YouTube videos of cute kittens and puppies
- Listening to someone talk about their problems – again and again
- Staring into space
- Doing tasks you could delegate to someone else (make the coffee, put the laundry on, pick up the dry cleaning, etc)

"If you want to make your dreams come true, the first thing you have to do is wake up."
~J.M. Power

Most of the reasons we've failed to achieve goals in the past can be eliminated quite easily. Taking control is about being solution oriented, and deciding to put yourself first (not by being detrimental to others, but prioritizing your needs, then focusing on others).

Taking control allows you to feel confident, empowered, and capable. No one wants to feel weak, disempowered or unhappy. Take charge of your life by setting realistic goals, quickly accomplishing small wins, and moving forward in a positive direction.

Goat setting and achieving allows you to feel in control of what goes on around you, demonstrating that proactive choices are possible, in regard to what you spend your time on.

Being A Better You

Achieving goals we set for ourselves can lead to many exciting areas of self improvement.

You may set specific personal development goals, or find that self improvement is a by product of other goals you set. For example, you may set a goal to learn self-defense, which is a great way to improve confidence, assertiveness, self-awareness, and fitness levels.

Or, you may simply learn to make a scrumptious chocolate cheesecake, which leads you to develop new skills and feel good about yourself.

> *"What you get by achieving your goals*
> *is not as important as what you*
> *become by achieving your goals."*
> *~ Zig Ziglar*

WHY BOTHER SETTING GOALS

Effective goal setting, and goal accomplishment, can lead to:

- New skills and unexpected abilities
- Improved social life
- Qualifications
- New opportunities
- Positive mindset
- Boost in confidence
- Lower stress levels
- Better health
- Eliminating fears and doubt
- Greater level of satisfaction in life
- Desire to learn more
- You're more fun to be around

SECRETS TO GOAL SETTING SUCCESS

The process of setting goals, accomplishing your task lists, and benefiting from the desired outcome, offers a great learning curve. It also provides opportunities to better yourself, plus, you have the chance to experience many of the fabulous rewards mentioned above.

Rather than question why we should bother with goals, it's more relevant to question why we wouldn't.

4

How To Be A Successful Goal Achiever

"Vision without action is a daydream.
Action without vision is a nightmare."
~Japanese Proverb

So far, we've looked at *what* goal setting is all about, and *why* goals are so powerful.

In this chapter, we'll look at *how* to achieve them, in an effortless and meaningful way.

As we discussed before, everyone has mini goals they set for themselves, whether they realize it or not. Here, we'll focus on specifically defined goals that provide us with forward momentum. We'll look at where to begin, how to capture the details you need, and what steps are required to carve out your ideal future.

Know Where You Are Today

POWER TIP 1 - Understanding exactly where you are today allows you to measure how far you've traveled at some relevant point in the future.

You may have reached a certain level in your academic education and would now like to progress further. You may have already achieved a specific set of creative skills or sporting ability, and now want to enhance those skills for pure enjoyment purposes.

Knowing where you are, and where you want to go, allows you to put measures in place to monitor your progress, and enthusiastically celebrate when you reach significant milestones.

With each goal you have in mind, take time out to review your current position, and make a note of any significant markers along the way to your desired outcome.

HOW TO BE A SUCCESSFUL GOAL ACHIEVER

*"If you don't know where you are going,
you'll end up someplace else."*
~ Yogi Berra

Re-train Your Brain

You may already be pumped, and about to race off and begin working on your goals. Or, you may be struggling to get started, and to the find inspiration or motivation you need.

If that's the case, then you're going to need to think and act differently.

*"Your altitude in life is determined
by your attitude,
not your aptitude"*
~ Zig Ziglar

Think differently

POWER TIP 2 - To really make progress, where you have previously struggled, or when you begin a new venture, you need a determined mindset.

As the famous saying goes "If you always do, what you've always done, you'll always get what you've always gotten." There are various reasons why goals can seem elusive or impossible. Examples include:

SECRETS TO GOAL SETTING SUCCESS

- Fear of failing
- Fear of success
- Self doubt
- Negative self talk
- Desire for perfectionism
- Concern about what others will think
- Blaming external events or circumstances
- Procrastination
- Lack of motivation

Tackle these issues, and you'll feel and act differently. Although that may not be as easy as it sounds, we all have the ability to change if we want to. This can mean the difference between wanting to move forward, but being stuck, and making massive progress.

This is a large subject to cover, much of which is beyond the scope of this book. However, some effective steps to help alter a *stuck* or *fearful* mindset can be:

- Commit to developing a positive attitude; read supportive self-help books.
- Banish negative self talk.
- Overpower imaginary obstacles.
- Hypnosis sessions to tackle deep seated issues.
- Meditation and relaxation techniques.

HOW TO BE A SUCCESSFUL GOAL ACHIEVER

- Know that you will encounter problems, but have faith you'll find solutions.
- Know that your brain will try to resist change, but persevere anyway.
- Have a clear plan to get from A to B, so you can follow the steps, without continually worrying about 'what ifs'.
- Create systems that allow you to move effortlessly through your task lists.
- Ignore the negative voices of others. If you want something badly enough, go for it regardless.
- Give yourself a shove, remind yourself *why* you want the end result, and get excited again.
- Take control, ignore what you can't control, and go for it.
- Believe you can achieve.

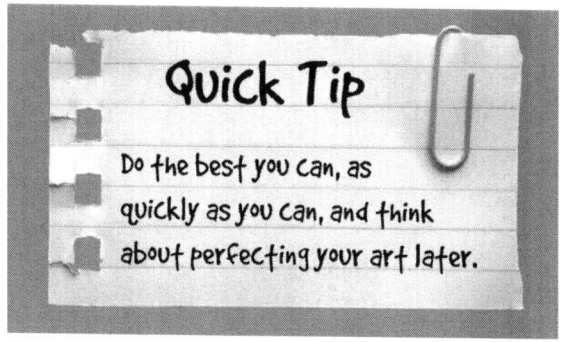

Quick Tip

Do the best you can, as quickly as you can, and think about perfecting your art later.

SECRETS TO GOAL SETTING SUCCESS

A change in your perspective and a positive, empowered attitude can do wonders. If you're held back by issues such as those above, seek support or keep trying to find solutions, so you can really take charge and create your ideal future.

Act differently

POWER TIP 3 - To receive the things you want, you need to act in certain ways. As is often said, 'Action speaks louder than words'.

Changing our way of thinking can be difficult, however, changing our *behavior* and choosing to act in specific ways can be an easier form of modification. When it comes to achieving your goals, success is far more likely when you take meaningful action. Below are some proactive examples of steps you could take:

- Write your goals down and read them daily.
- Share with the world, seek encouragement.
- Only use methods that work well for *you.*
- Complete at least one task each day, to move you closer to the desired outcome.
- Recognize the importance of each small step you take, and be grateful for the opportunity you were given to accomplish it.

HOW TO BE A SUCCESSFUL GOAL ACHIEVER

When you take positive action, things <u>will</u> change.

It's not about what you want, think about, or desire. Ultimately, it comes down to what you actually DO.

And, as a final note in this section, a key factor in succeeding with your goals is allowing your subconscious to work on them for you.

Our subconscious responds to whatever we feed it. Feed it with negative, self-defeating talk, and it will believe you. Feed it with positive, goal oriented, statements, and it will believe you.

When you build positive thinking habits (aligned to your goals and plans), and consistently reinforce these empowering messages, your subconscious will reward you. Not only will you be making conscious efforts to work toward your goals, but your subconscious mind will also support you with supportive, optimistic, and hopeful feelings.

"There are three kinds of people;
those who make things happen,
those who watch things happen,
and those who wonder what happened."
-Nicholas Butler Murray

SECRETS TO GOAL SETTING SUCCESS

Understand Where You Are Headed

POWER TIP 4 - Before you set your goals, it's important to appreciate where you are today.

If nothing changes, where will you be heading? What will life look like in 1, 5, 10, 25 years time? What has prevented, or is preventing, you from achieving your ideal situation?

> *"If you do not change direction,*
> *you may end up where you are heading."*
> *~ Lao Tzu*

Look at your life today, identify the goals that will create your ideal future, and understand what roadblocks could hold you back, or block your progress. Then, you're in a better position to create a workable plan that will make the all good stuff happen.

For example:

- Are you generally fit and healthy, but would now like to improve your heart rate, stamina, and muscle tone, to train for a triathlon?
- Are you unhappy with your current weight, which keeps creeping upward, and recognize

you need to lose X lbs to get back to a healthy level?

- Is your job boring, with limited prospects, but you have a vocational desire that requires you to get a specific qualification?
- Are you single, but would love to meet the person of your dreams and start a family?

Find what needs to change, remove the roadblocks, and create an action plan to accomplish those dreams.

Commitment And Motivation

How badly do you want the things you desire, and what will you do to get them?

SECRETS TO GOAL SETTING SUCCESS

Commitment

POWER TIP 5 - Let's start with commitment. By setting a goal, you're making a promise to yourself, and you should do everything possible to deliver a great result. **You owe it to yourself.**

> **Merriam-Webster dictionary definition:**
>
> *Commitment*
>
> : a promise to do or give something
> : a promise to be loyal to someone or something
> : the attitude of someone who works very hard to do or support something

You will no doubt make a strong commitment at the beginning of any goal setting process; however, you'll most likely need to re-commit on a regular basis. As much as a new goal can seem exciting to begin with, life can get in the way, may dampen your enthusiasm, or throw you off course.

When you find it hard to see the end any more, or become weighed down with other 'stuff', take time out to remind yourself *why* you started the journey, and to make a clear statement of intent to see it through.

HOW TO BE A SUCCESSFUL GOAL ACHIEVER

Motivation

POWER TIP 6 - Having the motivation to achieve something is one of the most significant factors in influencing a positive outcome.

> *"Motivation is when your dreams*
> *put on work clothes."*
> *~ Author Unknown*

Merriam-Webster dictionary definition:

Motivation

: the act or process of giving someone a reason for doing something: the act or process of motivating someone
: the condition of being eager to act or work: the condition of being motivated
: a force or influence that causes someone to do something

When you're enthusiastic and excited about a project, it seems anything is possible. However, you could also potentially get blown off course, distracted, or your enthusiasm becomes weakened along the way. Fortunately, there are many valuable tips to help you stay motivated. For example:

SECRETS TO GOAL SETTING SUCCESS

- Clearly visualize the outcome you desire, and the *feelings* you'll experience when you have achieved exactly what you want.
- Make sure you truly own the goal, that it's yours, not someone else's (unless you share the goal).
- Take consistent action – set realistic daily tasks, so you can see progress in action.
- Use positive self talk and affirmations.
- Quickly move past set-backs, and focus on the various mini achievements you've made to date.
- Prioritize significant tasks, focus on the important ones, and you'll feel a sense of achievement when they are ticked off the list.
- Seek support from enthusiastic people, who want to see you do well.
- Set deadlines for tasks to keep you on track, and to ensure constant momentum.
- Remember that persistence and determination *will* pay off.
- Reward yourself at pre-set milestones, or unexpected achievements.
- Use motivators such as uplifting music, motivational quotes or words, and pictures of your end goal.

HOW TO BE A SUCCESSFUL GOAL ACHIEVER

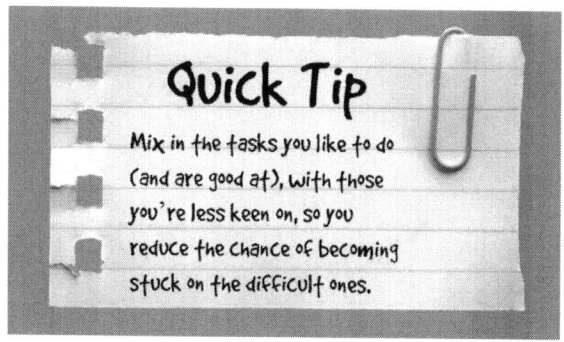

Mix in the tasks you like to do (and are good at), with those you're less keen on, so you reduce the chance of becoming stuck on the difficult ones.

Commitment and motivation are a powerful mix.

When you want something strongly enough, believe you're capable of achieving it, and back it up with significant action, **you can't fail to be successful!**

Prioritize And Choose Your Goals Carefully

POWER TIP 7 - Life is made up of both large and small goals. Selecting which ones are most important, and separating them from the irrelevant or insignificant ones is not always as easy as it sounds.

All too often, we find ourselves working on things that add very little value to our life, or to those we care about. These can range from projects for other people, to the daily detritus of stuff we are faced with.

SECRETS TO GOAL SETTING SUCCESS

"In absence of clearly defined goals, we become strangely loyal to performing daily acts of trivia."
~ Author Unknown

Stuff that eats into our time:

- Chatting to a neighbor for ages about nothing
- Wandering around the supermarket with no list
- Waiting in queues
- Opening post, admin tasks, paying bills, etc
- Chores, phone calls, texts, traffic jams, meal prep, and so forth

Projects we spend time on for others:

- Working late for the boss, with no specific benefit to you.
- Supporting a friend in their endeavors, but not receiving the same support from them.
- Supporting your spouse's career, putting your own plans on hold, but without future commitment toward your own desires.
- Running round for kids' activities, but not taking any time for yourself.

HOW TO BE A SUCCESSFUL GOAL ACHIEVER

Becoming involved with projects for other people can be very worthwhile. However, you need to ensure you still allow enough time, and energy, to focus on your own goals as well.

When we become weighed down with the daily barrage of jobs, tasks, and other people's needs, it can be distracting, and potentially time-wasting. Before you know it, you've lost days, weeks, months, or even years, without actively progressing toward your own dreams.

Prioritize

Prevent those losses from happening by creating a complete list of all the goals you'd like to work on, and then selecting the most important ones.

Write them all down, and review them slowly. Rate their importance, with 1 being the highest and 10 being the lowest.

Questions to ask yourself:

- What do I desire or think about most often?
- How do I feel when I envision myself achieving the goals – which outcomes *feel* the best?
- Do these goals reflect my values and purpose?
- Is the goal truly mine, or someone else's outcome they want for me?

SECRETS TO GOAL SETTING SUCCESS

- Does the goal fit with my lifestyle and skill set?
- Can I control the outcome?
- Are any of the goals urgent or an absolute must?
- Which short term goals can I complete easily?
- Which lifetime goals will add the most value to my life, and to those I care about?
- Which goals excite me the most?
- Is there something I want, but fear or doubt is holding me back?
- If I don't achieve the goal, will it matter?
- If I'm guaranteed not to fail, what will I do?

Another effective method to help choose your goals is to write down as many as you can possibly think of. From the large, audacious, scary, outrageous, and amazing ones, to the smaller, easier, safer, quicker ones. Write them down, whether they're exciting or boring, short or long term, personal or shared. Don't dismiss anything.

> *"Nobody succeeds beyond his or her wildest expectations unless he or she begins with some wild expectations."*
> *~ Ralph Charell*

Then, take a day to sleep on it, and review the list again. See which goals stand out as being the most motivating, the most important, or the most life changing. Are you more interested in the ones with long term objectives, or ones that will deliver quick wins?

Now, select only five from the list. That may take some time to think through, as there will likely be more than five that stand out. However, if you pick too many to start with, you're likely to become overwhelmed, lessening your chances of success with any of them. Just selecting five key goals (or less if you feel it's appropriate) will allow you to get moving quickly. As you complete some of the goals, you can always re-visit the list and select new ones, or replace them with fresh ones as your life goals change.

The goals you choose to spend you time on will help to define and create your future. Spend time and energy on unimportant ones, and you've missed a valuable opportunity to move closer to the things you truly find inspiring and enjoyable.

> Choose carefully, your future is
> in your hands!

Select Your Methods And Tools

Having goals is one thing, but being able to carry them out effectively, to get maximum results, is another.

SECRETS TO GOAL SETTING SUCCESS

The methods and tools you choose to work with, can often dictate the success of a goal. However, not all systems or tools will work for everyone, or in every circumstance. When you identify which method/s and tools resonate well with *you*, you've made a huge step in the right direction.

So, what options are there? The most popular method is the S.M.A.R.T. system, and then there are a number of techniques such as backward planning, daily to-do lists, picture boards and visualization.

Tools can include diaries, phone apps, software programs, worksheets, and action plans.

HOW TO BE A SUCCESSFUL GOAL ACHIEVER

S.M.A.R.T. Method

POWER TIP 8 - There are a number of word variations on the same theme, the one below being a popular version.

S – Specific
What exactly do you want to accomplish, why is it important to you, who can help, what requirements do you have, or issues you'll need to tackle

M – Measurable
Quantity, quality, distance, cost, etc. For example, how many are you aiming for, what did you start with, what is the number you require by the end?

A – Achievable (Attainable or Action Oriented)
Can you reasonably achieve this or are you attempting too much? Do you have the capability, finances, support, etc, to achieve the goal?

R – Relevant (Realistic)
Is the goal important to you, is this the right time, do you have the skills, energy, or time to commit to it?

T – Time-related (Trackable)
When does the goal need to be completed by, or what significant milestones are there along the way?

A working example could be:

Specific
- clearly outline what needs to be achieved

Learn to speak Spanish via evening classes, for a working vacation in Spain

Measurable
- identify a measurable outcome

Achieve a pass mark of 90% in the oral test, and 80% in the written test

Achievable
- can you commit to the task?

Six months of evening classes and homework

Realistic
- have you got resources & support you need?

Course fees, books, work rota agreed, to allow for study evenings

Time Specific
- when the goal needs to be achieved by

Complete the course by 30th April, ready for summer vacation in June

Setting effective goals takes practice. Using the S.M.A.R.T method is a relatively easy to follow thought process, which allows you to get a clear focus for *what* you want to achieve, *why* you want it, and *how* you'll get there (either with a detailed plan or just the outline steps).

<u>Backward Planning</u>

POWER TIP 9 - This can be a useful method in certain circumstances, especially for goals that are some distance away in the future. You begin with your end goal, and work systematically backward, to develop a plan.

Where a goal cannot be accomplished any time soon, understand the reasons why, and identify the steps required to bring it into reality.

Keep stepping backward, until you reach the tasks you can tackle *today*, which will signify your starting point. For example, if you've set your heart on becoming a Registered Nurse in the U.S., could you start working in the role today? Assuming you are not already qualified, then the answer is no, as you would need to pass the National Council Licensure Examination. Could you do that today? Not unless you have either a diploma, an Associate Degree in Nursing (ADN) or a Bachelor of Science in Nursing (BSN). Could you pass them today? Not unless you apply and get accepted onto a 2 or 4 year program. To get to that stage what steps need to be taken? Keep working the process backward, until there are no further steps to take.

SECRETS TO GOAL SETTING SUCCESS

Although a backward plan may appear similar to a traditional, forward based plan, it actually requires a different style of thinking. It can be a useful method to ensure that you haven't missed any critical steps, and to help clarify the timeline involved for a specific goal.

> *"When solving problems,*
> *dig at the roots instead of just*
> *hacking at the leaves."*
> *~ Anthony J. D'Angelo*

Picture boards

POWER TIP 10 - Some people respond best to visual stimulus. Vision boards, or action boards, can be a powerful method for creatively outlining, and recording your goals. You can create a dazzling array of photos and images that help bring to life the differing aspects of all your dreams and ambitions. For example, cut out colorful photos of your dream vacation, your ideal home, perfect job, happy lifestyle, and so on. Include uplifting quotes, your personal vision, positive thoughts, and anything you find inspiring, which reflects your desired outcome.

You can also create an action board or journal, to record in picture detail the successful steps you take toward achieving your goal. For example, you can pictorially record milestones on a calendar or diary, as

HOW TO BE A SUCCESSFUL GOAL ACHIEVER

you accomplish the various steps in your action plan. Visual prompts can include:

- A pin board covered with pictures from magazines, greeting cards, photos, brochures, inspiring quotes, or powerful words.
- Pinterest boards
- A diary or journal, filled with motivating pictures of your ideal future. You can update this with real photos of your achievements, at each key step you accomplish.
- Individual pictures or personal photos stuck to the refrigerator, bathroom mirror, study wall, etc. These could be photos of the tightly fitting dress you want slip into, the mountain top you want to reach, the layered wedding cake you want to make yourself, the dollar value you want to save, and so on.
- Inspirational photos kept in your bag or on your phone, that remind you daily of your awesome goal.

Be very clear on what you're trying to achieve. Create separate boards or collections, to reflect separate goals. Visual motivators should be fun – mess about and enjoy yourself!

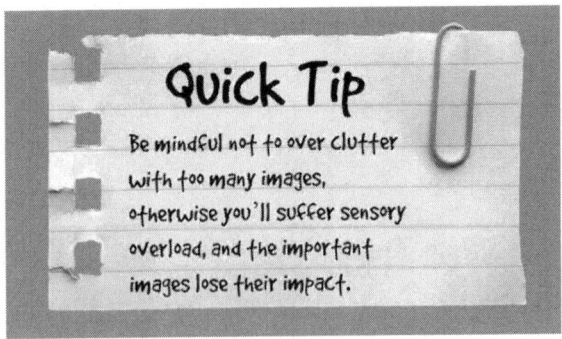

Visualization

POWER TIP 11 - To make a goal seem real, it helps to create an idea as to what the outcome looks and feels like. To visualizing the outcome, you create a clear mental picture of yourself having passed the finishing line of your goal. This helps to your brain to process positive thoughts and build a solid belief in the outcome.

"Visualize this thing you want.
See it, feel it, believe in it.
Make your mental blueprint and begin."
~ Robert Collier

There are two key areas of visualization – *outcome* based and *process* based. In the first, you create a strong mental image of what you see, hear, smell, taste, and feel, as you finally realize your goal. For example, if you want to learn how to create an oil painting, then you need to see yourself standing beside a beautiful, finished painting. What size frame is it in, what's the picture about, what colors jump out at you; notice the smell of the paint, and the positive comments from your friends when you show them. Imagine the pride you'll feel and the excitement, as you hang it on your wall at home.

Secondly, *process visualization* involves envisioning each of the steps you need to take to reach to your desired outcome. Don't focus on the actual goal, instead, picture yourself in detail at each of the key steps. To create your oil masterpiece, you will need to identify a suitable tutor, buy the relevant materials, attend lessons to learn the required skills, and so forth. Imagine the excitement of buying new paints, the feeling of the brush on the canvass, the voice of the tutor, the intense colors you mix, and the textures you're able to create.

Visualization may not work for everyone; however, it can be a very empowering method, delivering a range of benefits. For example, it can help to you:

- Feel in control of the process or outcome
- Lessen fears or doubts
- Feed positive messages to your subconscious
- Feel more focused
- Find fresh, new ideas
- Stay motivated

- Create solutions to problems
- Feel optimistic and happier

Successful achievement of goals may require a number of methods and tools to work together. Visualization techniques can be an effective way to create positive, helpful habits, and to keep your overall objective clear in the front of your mind.

Mind maps

POWER TIP 12 - Mind mapping is a large subject, beyond the scope of this book. However we have listed some further reading and software options in the resource and recommended reading sections toward the end of the book.

Mind maps can help to organize your goals, in a structured and visible way. We all have different learning styles, and for many people the process of working through a mind map is really useful.

Mind mapping can be a simple process, or highly complex, depending on the level you use it for. There are two main types of mind maps – paper based and computer generated. Hand written mind maps allow you to capture ideas as quickly as you think of them, plus, you can create images or designs however you please. Alternatively, software based mapping captures ideas in

HOW TO BE A SUCCESSFUL GOAL ACHIEVER

a more structured manner, retains the information for future adaptation, and allows you to share maps with others.

Creating a mind map starts by noting your main idea or strategy at the centre of the design, and working outward, building new layers of thought. Each new layer, or branch, can be identified using separate colors, arrows, shapes or other visuals means. The maps can be used at many levels, for example to capture all of your goals in one place, to breakdown a specific goal into manageable chunks, or to create simple to-do lists.

Example of basic mind map:

Benefits of mind mapping can include:

- Easy to create and adapt
- Avoids information becoming overwhelming
- Simple prioritization of tasks
- Opportunity to outline, test and explore your thought processes
- Clarity of connections and ideas, encouraging creativity
- Brainstorming with others
- Project planning and delegation
- Visually appealing and aids memory recall

Lists, lists, and lists

POWER TIP 13 - A fundamental method in goal achievement is creating a detailed plan. This can take various forms, such as mind maps, an implementation chart, diary, or good old fashioned lists.

Getting from A to B, whether you record it in detail or not, will involve incremental steps. Some people are good at memorizing stuff; others work better with a detailed action plan.

As you work your way through the plan, more of the small everyday tasks will appear, and it's important that you capture them as soon as you think of them.

HOW TO BE A SUCCESSFUL GOAL ACHIEVER

For example:

Goal – Learn to swim *plus* lose 10 pounds

- Make an appointment with a swimming coach at the local pool
- Select two suitable lesson times per week
- Buy new swimwear
- Research what to eat, and when to eat, before and after the swim session
- Start the day with 10 minutes stretching and 10 minutes cardiovascular exercises
- Reduce calorie intake on days with no swimming sessions
- Cut out processed sugars

When you're completely clear on your final goal, you can create a plan to achieve it. Larger goals will most likely need to be broken down into smaller, mini-goals, within the overall scheme. The added benefit of these small, mini-goals is that they act as great motivators along the way. As you tick them off the list, you can feel a sense of increasing pride at your achievements, and excitement at getting closer to the big dream.

There are many different ways to record your overall plans, or daily task lists. Tools to help you do this

SECRETS TO GOAL SETTING SUCCESS

can vary in complexity, from software based programs, to coaching programs, to smart phone apps, to plain old note pads or Post-it notes.

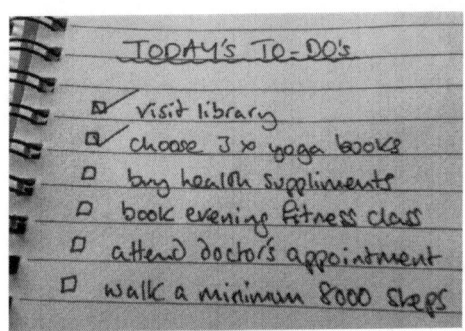

Pick the methods and tools that work best for you, and stick with them...

Effective Execution

POWER TIP 14 - Dreaming about your end goal is great; however, to get what you really want, you need an effective plan.

There are various smart ways to execute your plans; you just need to pick ones that will help you achieve the best results, in the most efficient and effective manner.

There are no absolutely right or wrong ways to work on your goals, although there are bad behaviors, or habits, which will hold you back and prevent you from progressing. Listed below are some of the more

HOW TO BE A SUCCESSFUL GOAL ACHIEVER

powerful steps you can take to ensure you have a robust plan and a solid approach to your goal.

- **Check for conflict** - goals should not conflict with each other, or be unrealistic e.g., you won't be able to drop 2 dress sizes in 2 months, if your weight management goal is to only lose 2 lbs a month.

- **Set <u>positive</u> goals**, using positive language. Instead of saying you 'want to leave your boring job', change your words to say you 'want to get a new, more interesting job'. Avoid focusing on what you *don't* want; always focus on what you *do* want.

- **Identify performance related goals**, as opposed to outcome based goals. An outcome may be affected by circumstances outside of your control, such as the weather, a co-workers health, or traffic delays. Your personal performance, however, is strictly under your control. This allows you to focus on areas that you can personally take charge of, and therefore feel pleased with your own performance; for example, making 20 sales calls, as opposed to making 5 actual sales.

- **Divide and conquer.** A large, overall goal can seem unobtainable, too much effort, or too far away. Smaller mini-goals are much more achievable, and you'll be surprised at how quickly you can tick things off the list.

- **Write them down** – this will help you to be precise with your objective (remember S.M.A.R.T?), and it enables you to track your progress. Areas to create mini-goals will then become obvious, plus, you can highlight your progress along the way, and enjoy greater satisfaction throughout the process.

- **Be clear on your priorities.** Most likely, you'll be working on a number of goals, or task lists (even task lists not related to any specified goal). Each day, identify the most important tasks from your lists, and get them done early. That way, you'll consistently make progress on the areas that matter most, and more likely to retain your motivation and focus.

- **Keep it simple** – don't try to do too much all at once – you know what'll happen! Identify simple systems and tools to support your efforts, and don't over complicate things.

- **Keep them front-of-mind.** Goals can easily get lost when life gets in the way. Keep them physically in sight, by using motivating pictures in prominent places, keep your to-do list on top

of your in-tray, set reminders on your phone, and so on. Don't bury them!
- **Take daily action.** You may not always be able to set aside hours to work on your goals, but even the smallest of actions can help you move forward. Be clear on your task lists, and be creative with what you need to do – even if it's only one quick phone call, one email responded to, one chapter read, one healthy eating habit achieved, one flight of stairs you run up, and so forth.

Focus on being effective and efficient with your time. Do this in a consistent manner, and small steps each day will build up, to make a substantial difference.

*"Discipline is the bridge between goals
and accomplishment."*
~ Jim Rohn

Get Organized

POWER TIP 15 - Becoming organized may sound scary but it can be simple and fun, and will lead to some great results.

Good time management skills will help you stay on top of your tasks and to get more done, without feeling

SECRETS TO GOAL SETTING SUCCESS

overwhelmed. Although it can require discipline, the benefits are well worth the effort.

It's all about knowing your priorities, being laser focused, and using simple, effective tools.

Simple organizational steps for successful goal achievement:

- **Select your best system and tools.** Do you like to work with pen and paper, smart phone apps, software programs, chalk boards, Post-it notes, etc? Pick the wrong ones, and you'll confuse yourself. Keep it simple and do what works for you.

> TODAY'S MUST DO'S
> ~~make appoint with doctor~~
> get blender for smoothie making
> collect pedometer
> ~~shop for organic fruit & veg~~
> get 8 hours sleep!

HOW TO BE A SUCCESSFUL GOAL ACHIEVER

- **Set a clearly defined goal**, outline your plan, and break it down into manageable chunks. Then, work out your daily to-do list.
- **Clear a work area.** Clutter can distract and derail you. If you can't or won't eliminate general clutter, find a place where you can create a temporary clear area. You can then place yourself into a positive zone, and focus solely on your goal tasks.
- **Be unavailable.** In a section below, we outline steps for removing distractions. Part of being organized is to ensure that you allocate time to achieve the tasks you've promised yourself you'll complete. Excuse yourself if necessary, and be unavailable for a short period. Lock yourself in the car, shed, or bathroom if necessary!
- **Pick one thing** – select the most important thing on your task list, and complete it, come hell or high water.
- **Get it done early.** Allocate time and attention to your goal's task list, as early as possible each day. That way, you'll achieve what you need to, and can allow the rest of the day to be about other 'stuff'.
- **Practice.** Time management skills and achieving high levels of productivity is not always easy. If you struggle to get things done, or feel that you

could do better, there are many books and online tools that can help. Don't allow poor organizational skills to block you from achieving your goals.

With a systematic approach, and a positive attitude, you will increase your chances of successfully completing each of the goals you set yourself. Plus, you'll achieve them in a fast and enjoyable manner.

Fight Fear And Doubt

POWER TIP 16 - Experiencing fear and doubt, in relation to your goals, or the tasks involved to reach them, is perfectly normal. Your ability to control, and overcome, these fears is what's important.

> *"If you put everything off till you're sure of it, you'll get nothing done."*
> *~ Norman Vincent Peale*

There are many reasons why people suffer from insecurities, and allow self-doubt to take hold. Examples can be:

- I'm too old
- I'm too young

HOW TO BE A SUCCESSFUL GOAL ACHIEVER

- I don't have enough education
- It will take too long
- I never have enough time
- What if I fail
- What will others think of me
- I'm not intelligent enough
- I don't have the necessary resources
- I'm not healthy enough
- I'm too shy or insecure
- It's too risky

The reality is, most of these fears are imagined, and can become an excuse for inaction. We naturally avoid pain and discomfort; therefore, if we perceive that a specific action will be uncomfortable for us, we'll find ways to avoid it.

The dilemma with that is, you'll never move past the problem, and therefore won't progress toward your desired outcome.

The good news is that there are solutions to managing fears and self doubt:

- Know that it's normal to feel that way.
- Make a list of your fears, and all the areas you can think of that are worrying you.

SECRETS TO GOAL SETTING SUCCESS

- Accept that there are solutions, and that you'll find them when you begin to look
- Get busy, start to take some steps toward your goal, and you'll notice the thing you fear is not nearly as bad as you thought it was.
- Use positive language. Don't say to yourself "I'm bound to fail"; instead, say, "If it doesn't work this time, I'll try another way". Avoid negative words such as *'can't, won't, fail, never, I'm not...'* Instead use positive phrases such as *'can, will, try, shall, positive'*
- Once you begin to tackle the things you're scared of, you'll feel empowered, and find that your confidence grows.
- Check that the goal is actually realistic – if not, it could be that your fears and doubts are justified. Set a new, realistic goal to work on instead.
- Take action – make a decision, be bold, go for it!

"To think too long about doing a thing often becomes its undoing."
~ Eva Young

Decide on how *much* you want to reach your goal. If you keep making excuses, and let fear hold you back, then you probably don't want it enough.

Go back to your list of goals, and check that you've chosen ones you're genuinely motivated to work on. If you are completely motivated, you'll find a way to bypass any fears.

And, of course,
you can always set a goal to
overcome your fears!

Eliminate Distractions And Obstacles

POWER TIP 17 - We all get interrupted and sidetracked every day. From the unexpected phone call, to the dog being sick as you leave for work, to the headache that keeps you from concentrating.

And then, there are the obstacles that fall in our path – the puncture that held you up for hours, the loss of important documents, the redundancy notice, or a bout of ill health.

*"We are kept from our goal
not by obstacles but by a
clear path to a lesser goal."*
~ Robert Brault

SECRETS TO GOAL SETTING SUCCESS

How you handle these issues is the key to preventing them from sabotaging your goals. Tackle them swiftly, and they will be behind you. Have a clear, well organized set of tasks for the day, and you'll gain your focus back quickly.

"One of the secrets of life is to make stepping stones out of stumbling blocks."
~Jack Penn

Be mindful of your own distraction weaknesses:

- Excessive use of social networks
- Chatting for ages
- Watching pointless TV programs

HOW TO BE A SUCCESSFUL GOAL ACHIEVER

- Indecision and procrastinating
- Over committing to others
- Taking on too much work
- Poor organization
- Over planning and worrying
- Allowing interruptions to take too long
- Grasshopper mind, with thoughts bouncing all over the place

We can't always prevent the obstacles that fall in our way, but we can control the annoying distractions. It's unlikely that we can remove them completely; however, we can efficiently and effectively manage them, to allow us more time and energy for our goals, and to spend time on things we enjoy.

Control your time-stealers:

- **Ban technology** when you need to work on your list. No emails, mobile, TV, etc. Set this in place for a short time, while you concentrate. You *will* survive without them.
- **Be unavailable.** Let people know that you're not available for a specific period of time, as you complete your important tasks. Let them know

that once you've finished, they have your complete attention.

- **Gather all the required information**, before you begin a task. It will save you wasting time and needing to start again.

- **Be clear on your objectives** before you begin a task. Know what you want to achieve, plan it carefully and land the result you need, quickly.

- **Be a decision maker.** When you procrastinate, you waste time. Make decisions fast, trust your instincts. Better to make a decision than no decision at all.

- **Learn to say 'no'** to others, when their requests conflict with your objectives. You can always agree on an alternative or a compromise, without allowing your own tasks to suffer.

- **Manage your time sensibly.** You can't do everything, and you can't be all things to all people. Attempt too much and you'll struggle to progress. Be selfish occasionally, and make time for the tasks that are important to you.

- **Get organized.** Don't let poor systems, lost paperwork, or an unclear strategy waste your time.

- **Take a break.** You can easily lose productivity or focus if you work on something for too long. If you begin to feel yourself drifting, becoming slow or struggling to make progress, take a break. Get some fresh air, a change of scenery, a new focus, etc. Even a quick 'time-out' can help pep up your productivity.

- **Analyze your behavior.** If you still feel as though you are losing time to distractions, analyze how you spend your time over a couple of days. Find the culprits, and commit to reducing their impact.

- **Learn to delegate.** Can someone else take on some chores? Can other people at work complete tasks that don't support your promotion prospects? Is it better to call the plumber than try and fix the leaky tap yourself?

*"Life's problems wouldn't be called "hurdles"
if there wasn't a way to get over them."
~ Author Unknown*

Learning to manage distractions is an extremely powerful skill to develop. You will benefit in so many ways. You'll gain more time to focus on your goals, and to spend on the things you enjoy. You'll feel more in control, and you'll gain confidence in your ability to achieve more.

Life throws up unexpected challenges all the time. It's our ability to meet, and overcome those challenges that determines our success in life.

New Helpful Habits

> *"First we make our habits,*
> *then our habits make us."*
> *~ Charles C Noble*

POWER TIP 18 - To be successful at achieving your goals, you'll need to develop some helpful, goal-oriented habits.

Research has demonstrated that it can take at least 21 days to develop a new habit. Changing lifelong habits can be hard work; however, building *new* daily habits for goal achievement can be an empowering activity that's extremely worthwhile.

Everyone has the desire to improve themselves or their lives at some point. Most of us would like to benefit from improved health, relationships, finances, lifestyle and general levels of happiness.

The goals we choose to set ourselves can help us to achieve those desires. However, it's using the correct set of regular habits and behaviors that will turn these into a reality.

HOW TO BE A SUCCESSFUL GOAL ACHIEVER

**So, the question is:
what helpful habits do we need,
and how do we set them to autopilot?**

Simple, supportive habits:

- **Daily habits** can be the quickest to identify and to create.

- **Be precise** about what you expect of yourself, e.g., 'I will drink a healthy smoothie for breakfast each morning, before leaving the house'.

- **Set benefit based habits**, e.g., learn to delegate at least one task a day, so *you* have more time to do what you need.

- **Make them easy and repeatable.** For example, ban yourself from using social media, texting friends, or any other social distractions until you've at least achieved the most important task on your list for the day.

- **One step at a time** – if you try to change, or start too many habits at the same time, you're less likely to succeed than if you begin with one or two helpful habits. Focus intently on them, until they are on auto-pilot.

SECRETS TO GOAL SETTING SUCCESS

- **Keep a daily chart**, for at least 21 days, so you can reinforce the new behavior, and track your success.

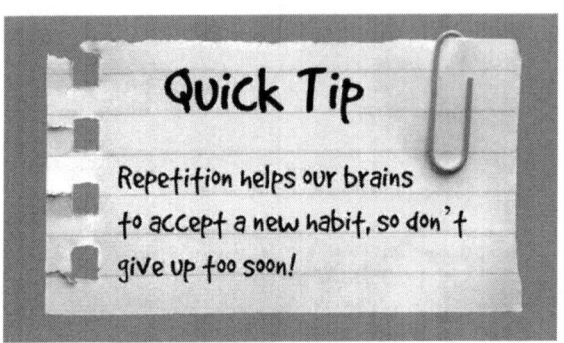

Once you have a clear objective in mind, helpful goal habits can be easy to identify, and implement. For example, if you set a goal to lose weight, then the following daily habits could be helpful:

- Park twice as far from the office as normal, so you walk further, and use a pedometer to track your daily steps.
- Use the stairs, not the lift.
- Select a smaller dinner plate to limit your portion size.
- Eat a small, healthy breakfast to prevent unhealthy snacking later in the day.

- Drink at least 2 liters of water throughout the day.
- No snacking in the evening, after 7pm.
- Set up a calorie counter on your phone, to check portion sizes, and nutritional content.

Many goals can be supported by implementing small, manageable habits. Look through your plans and task lists, and see if there are any helpful habits you could set in place. Once you practice these for a few weeks, they'll be set to auto-pilot, leaving you mind space for the other more complicated, or one-off things on your list.

"Sow a thought, and you reap an act;
Sow an act, and you reap a habit;
Sow a habit, and you reap a character;
Sow a character, and you reap a destiny."
~ Samuel Smiles

Maintain Forward Momentum

POWER TIP 19 - Remember the time when you were out with friends, excitedly chatting about a new travel/business/family plan you had? Or the time you went for a long, thoughtful, walk, and decided on a new direction you were going to take your life in?

Then, before you knew it, a year passed by and you'd barely got anything started? That's been the reality at some point or other for most of us. The question is, how do you sustain the level of excitement you first felt about your goal, prevent distractions and obstacles de-railing you, and retain your focus?

- **Do a daily to-do.** Even a small, 2 minute activity, can give you a sense of achievement, and keep your goal front-of-mind.

- **Keep up the power habits.** Your helpful habits are powerful because they drive you forward methodically, and then automatically. Tick them off on a daily chart, or place prominent reminders somewhere you can't ignore them.

- **Forward plan your milestones.** Make a note of when you expect to achieve specific stages of your goal, and check in with yourself. If you're ahead of schedule, congratulate yourself. If you're behind schedule, reevaluate the timeline and tasks involved, and reset the schedule.

- **Share your goals** and key milestones with others, and ask for their support. Having someone cheer you on, or bail you out if things get tough, can be invaluable.

- **Don't goal hop.** Exercise self discipline and stay focused on your chosen goals. Don't be tempted to hop around into new, easier, or more exciting projects, each time something presents itself. Practice self discipline, and you will see results soon enough, allowing you to set those shiny, new goals. Jumping around means you'll likely struggle to finish anything!

- **Check your motivation.** If you've lost enthusiasm for the goal, you need to understand why. Maybe the goal is something you no longer want to peruse, for genuine reasons. Maybe you've hit a roadblock, and just need to find a way round. Or, may be you need some time out, to refresh and re-energize yourself.

- **Check that your systems, tools and organizational methods are supportive** and not holding you back. If you struggle with them, they may not be the right ones for you. Swap them for ones that will benefit you, rather than hinder you.

- **Believe in your success.** Those who believe they will succeed are far more likely to do so than those who don't.

*"focus on the front windshield
and not the review mirror"
~ Colin Powell*

Your ability to maintain focus on key tasks and objectives, for both short and long periods, can be difficult, and requires a certain level of self discipline.

If your goals are important enough to you, you will find a way to keep them in focus. Persistence will pay off in the long run, so find a way to maintain your helpful habits, remove distractions or roadblocks, stay energized, and keep a spotlight on your awesome goal.

Stop And Review

POWER TIP 20 - Sometimes you need to slow down, and take a look at where you are. Take stock of what you've achieved so far, and if something's not working, find out why, and reset the goal, if necessary.

HOW TO BE A SUCCESSFUL GOAL ACHIEVER

Let's face it, if you don't stop to review, how do you know if you're making progress, heading in the right direction, or on target?

Reviews don't need to be too formal, just regular enough to check in with yourself, and be happy that everything is on track. For example, you could review at set points, e.g., weekly, or maybe each time you reach a pre-set milestone. Do whatever works for you, and allows you to put everything into perspective.

Take time to check:

- If you learn things along the way that mean you need to change the plan, don't fret about it, just do it.
- Change happens, circumstances change, we change as we mature, and so do our needs and desires. Our goals may need to be altered or replaced to reflect these changes.
- If you find you lack necessary skills to progress, stop, learn them, or find someone who can carry out those required tasks for you.
- Don't give up at the first sign of difficulty. Persevere. Adapt. Remember how you'll *feel* when you've accomplished the goal.
- If you feel overwhelmed, take time out. Stress and anxiety will hold you back. Review, and

SECRETS TO GOAL SETTING SUCCESS

pause things where possible, so you can catch up with yourself. Nothing's worth making yourself ill over.

- Are you still clear on where you're going, and how to get there? If things are becoming confused or you're heading off path, regular reviews allow you to take control again.

- Is the goal still realistic? Check in with your S.M.A.R.T. notes, and refresh your memory, or reevaluate if necessary.

- Be proud of what you've achieved so far.

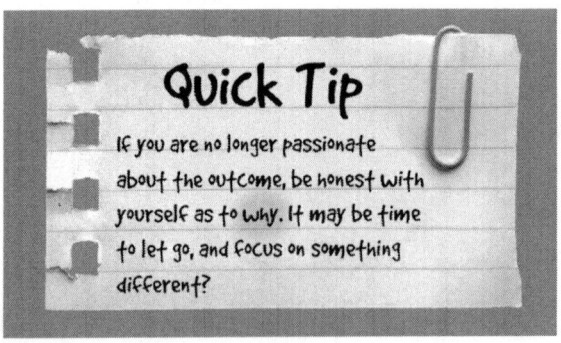

Quick Tip

If you are no longer passionate about the outcome, be honest with yourself as to why. It may be time to let go, and focus on something different?

When you take time out to review your goals, you also help to etch them further on to your subconscious. This, in turn, helps to lessen any confusion you might be feeling, and to prevent you from becoming lost somewhere along the way.

HOW TO BE A SUCCESSFUL GOAL ACHIEVER

"Fall seven times,
Stand up eight."
~ Japanese Proverb

If you do become stuck, review your S.M.A.R.T. plan, and try asking yourself some of the following:

- Is your ultimate objective still that same?
- Are you comfortable with the direction you're heading?
- Are there better ways to strengthen, or modify your original plans?
- Are your systems and tools supportive?
- Do you have enough helpful habits in place?
- What new skills could you benefit from?
- Is there someone, or something, that could help you achieve more, in less time?
- Do you still feel motivated by the final outcome?
- Is your goal developing into something new, or larger, and does your plan need to be adjusted?

Questions such as these allow you to analyze your current and future situation. They put you firmly back in control.

So, stop and review regularly. If it's working, do more of it, if not, modify or try new ways. Certainly don't waste time, or mental energy worrying about *what-if's*. Stay in focus, and maintain the momentum.

Milestones And Rewards

Milestones

POWER TIP 21 - Goals specify what you want, and where you're going. Milestones act as markers, to signify you're on the right path to getting what you want.

Milestones allow you to easily see your progress. It can take less effort to adjust your plans between milestones, and to visualize the tasks required between each milestone, than to try and see all the way to the end of your goal.

Milestones can also be seen as mini-goals in themselves, with their own action plan for achieving them. For example:

Main Goal – clear credit card debts and start saving toward a deposit for your own home.

- **Milestone 1** – pay off 1st credit card within 6 months.
- **Milestone 2** – Open an interest based savings account, and make 1st deposit (starting the helpful habit of monthly deposits, albeit small, until debt is clear).

HOW TO BE A SUCCESSFUL GOAL ACHIEVER

- **Milestone 3** – pay off 2nd credit card within 18 months.
- **Milestone 4** – set up small everyday savings account for emergencies and cut up credit cards!
- **Milestone 5** – identify amount required for house deposit and save, save, save until target amount reached.

Milestone markers can be set at whatever stage of the plan you think is appropriate. They could present themselves at certain time-bound stages of your plan, such as when you've paid off a specific credit card. Or, they could be set against a measurable, for example, when you have run you're first half marathon, in the training program for a full marathon.

> Another powerful method, when using milestones, is to capture momentous moments as they happen.

For example, you could:

- Frame the dollar bill given to you by your first paying customer.
- Print out your first blog post that went viral.

SECRETS TO GOAL SETTING SUCCESS

- Pin your credit card statement, showing a zero balance, to the wall, with a happy, smiley photo of yourself.
- Frame your hard-won certificates, and display them proudly.
- Keep a photo on your phone of you, as you cross the finish line of your half marathon, so the next step doesn't feel out of reach...

Milestones allow you to set stepping stones along the way, and to gain a sense of satisfaction, and belief, that that overall goal is definitely in sight. They also help you to be flexible, and make small adjustments as required, before you get too far along the journey.

Rewards

POWER TIP 22 - A major motivator between the start and completion of your goal, especially for long-term goals, is to recognize and reward your successes along the way.

> *"Celebrate what you want*
> *to see more of."*
> *~ Tom Peters*

HOW TO BE A SUCCESSFUL GOAL ACHIEVER

Achieving goals should be fun, and you should celebrate your mini-achievements, as much as the major ones. Even the smallest amounts of progress are still a victory.

Unfortunately, negative emotions can play their part as you work toward your goals, including disappointment, frustration, fear, anger, self recrimination, apathy, and so on. Therefore, you need to make the most of the positive opportunities when they present themselves.

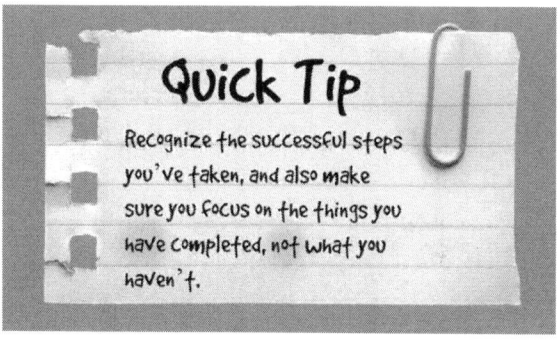

There are many, many ways to recognize and reward how fabulous you are. For example:

- Buy yourself that tempting new paperback, and snuggle down for the next few evenings, getting lost in the world of your favorite author.

SECRETS TO GOAL SETTING SUCCESS

- If you've been overly absorbed in your goal recently, take time out do something fun with friends or your family.
- Small victories = small rewards. Pop out for a walk in the fresh spring air, pick up your favorite chocolate candy, or an indulgent magazine you can dive into that evening.
- Pre-set a date for a vacation, a long weekend away, or a day pampering at the spa, when you expect to achieve a major milestone.
- Give yourself a pat on the back and say well done!

Remember to stop along the journey, and take time to enjoy the sense of satisfaction as you complete a difficult task, or overcome an unexpected roadblock.

Life is too short not to have fun. Your achievements become even more special, when you recognizing how much they've enhanced your skills, helped you make new friends, revealed something new about yourself, built your confidence, and have demonstrated you that you *do* have the self discipline and ability to achieve whatever you want.

"The more you praise and celebrate your life, the more there is in life to celebrate."
~ Oprah Winfrey

Worksheets And Resources

Everyday goals are generally easy to achieve. Get up at a certain time, help the kids with their homework each day, put the laundry on before you leave for work, eat a protein rich breakfast, remember to listen when other speak, and so on.

However, when it comes to the bigger, long-term goals, we need a robust strategy and plan of attack. Knowing what you want may not be enough. Having a set of inspirational tools to help you get there can often be the catalyst to turning your dreams in to a reality.

Goal Setting Worksheets, or Planners, are valuable because they force you to be clear and precise. They help you capture the essentials, to be efficient, and to stay on course.

Examples of inspirational tools could be:

- S.M.A.R.T. Planners.
- Done-for-you Worksheets.
- Customizable Planners, so you can adapt them to suit your personal preferences.
- Progress Sheets for vision, goals, plans, milestones, and tasks.
- Goal Checklists, with check boxes to capture your progress.

SECRETS TO GOAL SETTING SUCCESS

- Goal identifiers, to capture key areas, e.g., finances, family, career, recreation, etc.
- Huge calendar, for interactive family involvement.
- Mind mapping software
- Personalized journal, to note the successful steps, or any challenges you've overcome, during your journey.

These tools help us, and those around us, to see the big picture, plus, the small details. Not only are we able to clearly see *what*, and *why*, but also *how*, as we work through a manageable action plan.

Resources

There are many helpful online resources available, with some requiring a payment, although many are free. Below we've listed a few of the better known ones. Depending on your preferred style for capturing and working on your goals, they may be worth checking out.

www.goal-buddy.com - Free online tool helping you to set goals, build new habits and manage task lists. Simple, easy to use, and clear to see your actions in progress. Includes email or SMS reminders as required.

HOW TO BE A SUCCESSFUL GOAL ACHIEVER

www.joesgoals.com - Free online tool showing a daily and weekly snapshot of goals. Useful for habit building or repetitive goals, and includes a daily logging option. Not so relevant for building changeable task lists.

https://asana.com - Free online program, ideal for sharing projects with others (or using as an individual). Captures goals and separates tasks for all team members. Enables easy communication, and allows a clear overview plus the capturing of relevant details.

www.mindmaple.com – Free online tool to create mind maps for business, education and personal use.

www.lifetick.com - Various pricing levels, with a 14 days free trial. Available for PCs, iphone, ipad and Android. Good for utilizing the S.M.A.R.T. method, allowing you to create detailed task lists and set reminders. Also includes personalized tracking, charts and reports.

Additionally, there are a huge range of apps you can download to your phone or tablet. Again, these maybe worth looking into, as you might find some that perfectly match your personal requirements.

SECRETS TO GOAL SETTING SUCCESS

Worksheets

We've created some example worksheets, which you may find helpful. The templates are shown on the following pages, or to access PDF copies please visit our website – www.feelfabtoday.com/goal-achievements. The templates can be printed out, or used as they are, or adapted to suit your own specific purposes.

Example worksheets:

- Goal Selection Worksheet
- S.M.A.R.T. Goals Worksheet
- Goals - Step by Step Worksheet
- Goals - Weekly To-Do List
- Goal Task List

HOW TO BE A SUCCESSFUL GOAL ACHIEVER

goalselectionworksheet

Identify at least three motivating goals for each category.

Job/career/business	Self Improvement	Health & Wellness
1/	1/	1/
2/	2/	2/
3/	3/	3/

Friends & Family	Finances	Religious or Spiritual
1/	1/	1/
2/	2/	2/
3/	3/	3/

Personal Relationships	Fun	Home
1/	1/	1/
2/	2/	2/
3/	3/	3/

Now, select the top five, most important goals, to work on as a matter of priority.

My top five goals that matter the most

1/
2/
3/
4/
5/

goalselectionworksheet provided courtesy of www.feelfabtoday.com

SECRETS TO GOAL SETTING SUCCESS

goalsworksheet
stepbystep

Divide your vision, goal and milestones into manageable parts, with separate plans and tasks for each milestone.

Vision – vividly detail your overall aim or desire. Describe what you see in your mind when you visualize the outcome of your goal.

Goal – specifically detail the outcome you desire. Check that it's specific, measurable, achievable, realistic and time bound.

Milestones – identify significant milestones that mark an important stage in your progress toward your desired outcome.

Plan per milestone – identify the key steps required to arrive at the **first** or **next** milestone.

HOW TO BE A SUCCESSFUL GOAL ACHIEVER

Tasks – list all the relevant tasks involved to complete the plan for the chosen milestone.

Repeat the process for each milestone, and you will clearly and easily move closer and closer toward achieving your goal.

goalsworksheet provided courtesy of www.feelfabtoday.com

SECRETS TO GOAL SETTING SUCCESS

s.m.a.r.t.goalsworksheet

Complete the boxes below for each goal you set yourself.
Date started _____

S
- **Specific** – state exactly what you want to achieve (who, what, when, where, why).

M
- **Measurable** – how will you assess your progress (how much, how many, how far)?

A
- **Achievable** – Do you have the skills, support or time required? Can you control it?

R
- **Realistic** – is it practical given the resources, time and knowledge available?

T
- **Timely** – state when you expect to see a result. Include dates, frequency and deadlines.

s.m.a.r.t.goalsworksheet provided courtesy of www.feelfabtoday.com

HOW TO BE A SUCCESSFUL GOAL ACHIEVER

SECRETS TO GOAL SETTING SUCCESS

Monday	Tuesday	Wednesday	Thursday	Friday	Saturday	Sunday

Weekly to-do list

Side Notes

weeklyto-dolist provided courtesy of www.feelfabtoday.com

HOW TO BE A SUCCESSFUL GOAL ACHIEVER

Exercises And Action Points

Goal setting is never the exciting part, goal *achieving* is. You'll save yourself massive amounts of time and effort, and will accomplish your goals faster and more easily, when you use effective methods, that are proven to work for *you*.

Below are some supportive exercises to smoothly guide you through the thought processes required for effective goal setting. Their relevance may depend on where you are specifically in your goal setting journey. Pick the ones that add the most value to you, and fill in the blanks.

Exercise 1 – Being S.M.A.R.T.

Carefully read each of the statements in the boxes on the following page, and think about what's required to complete the blank space beneath each question, for each of your goals. If you can't answer the questions quickly, spend some time considering the answer, and re-visit again later.

SECRETS TO GOAL SETTING SUCCESS

SPECIFIC State exactly WHAT you want to achieve. (who, what, when, where, why)

MEASURABLE How will you assess your progress (how much, how many, how far?)

ACHIEVABLE Is it feasible? Do you have the skills & time required? Can you control it?

REALISTIC Is it practical, given the resources, time & knowledge available?

TIMELY State WHEN you expect to see a result. Include dates, frequency & deadlines.

HOW TO BE A SUCCESSFUL GOAL ACHIEVER

Exercise 2 – How To Choose

Grab yourself a sheet of paper or a notepad. Write down everything you would like to achieve. *Everything.* Big, small, one-off, repetitive, boring, weird, exciting, easy, complicated, selfish, unselfish, cheap, expensive, immediate, lifelong, and so forth. Cover all the areas of your life; family, friends, career, education, health, hobbies, finances, and any areas that stand out as important. *Write it all down.*

Now sleep on it.

Review the list with fresh eyes the next day. Add to it if you've thought of other items. Now, ask yourself – if you could only achieve five of the items on the list, which five would you pick?

They're the ones you should be working on. Now go and get started…

SECRETS TO GOAL SETTING SUCCESS

Exercise 3 – Get Emotional!

Answer the questions below honestly, and see how they make you feel. Do the answers influence your thoughts toward the goals you should *really* be working on?

Negative Emotions	Positive Emotions
What makes me sad, angry, frustrated, upset, fearful or lack confidence?	What makes me truly happy, proud, excited, determined and inspired for the future?
What am I currently doing that is insignificant?	What matters to me most?
Is there anything I really dislike about my life right now?	What do I love to do?
What do I need to do to change this?	What do I need to do, to feel those emotions more often?

HOW TO BE A SUCCESSFUL GOAL ACHIEVER

Now, think about the following:

- Imagine you could achieve all the goals you ever thought possible. Picture yourself as having achieved all the outcomes you desire. After successfully completed your goals, how does it make you feel?
- If you were guaranteed not to fail, what goals would you work on?
- What therefore, should you stop focusing on, that currently prevents you from working on those goals?

What should you start doing today, to move closer to your ideal future?

Exercise 4 – Horrible Or Helpful Habits

As we've seen in the earlier section on *new habit forming*, our habits can make or break us. Invest some time to explore how *your* current habits either support or hinder both your short and long term goals. Then, evaluate what you could do differently, starting today.

Current **unhelpful** habits	New, replacement, **helpful** habits

Exercise 5 - System Support

In the past, what goal systems or tools have you used? Did they work well or did they hold you back?

Could you benefit from a stronger set of tools, to make your life easier, and, therefore, your goals become more attainable?

If so, have you checked out the tools that are available online, on your phone, in the shops, or that you could simply create yourself? Spend some time searching through the assorted options, and pick out ones you think will work best for *you*.

Make a list of three supportive tools you'll put in place, now that you have a new perspective on goal setting.

1._____

2._____

3._____

SECRETS TO GOAL SETTING SUCCESS

Exercise 6 – Visionary Moments

Create a vision and action board this weekend.

Simply pick up a poster board, some relevant magazines or images, and some glue or pins.

Think about the perfect vision you have for the future, and the specific goals you need to accomplish so you can turn your dreams into reality. Select motivational images that represent your desires, and the steps you'll need to take.

For example, if you want to own your own coffee shop, select pictures of a thriving coffee shop, happy customers, a till stuffed with money, beautiful drinks, a smiling you. Add in quotes you find inspirational, and anything that represents specific milestones you need to reach. Include statements of intent, such as *"I will open 'Candy's Coffee and Cake Emporium' twelve months from today"*. When you look at your board, it should make you feel super excited, and hopeful for the future.

These pictorial prompts can act as powerful tools to keep you focused on what you *really* want, and what you have to do to get there.

Go play around, have fun, and see what the future can look like!

Exercise 7 – Lay It Out

Practice laying out the steps you'll need to take to finally achieve your goal. Use the example template below to insert each of your own goals. This can work for both large and small goals, and is useful for breaking goals down into manageable, easy-to-see steps.

Vision
To own a coffee shop chain, with a minimum 6 units, within 30 miles of home, in the next 5 years.

Goal (1st of many)
Open 1st unit in my home town, within 12 months

Milestones
Create and present business plan
Loan approved
1st location identified and completed
Supplier's agreements confirmed
Staff hired
Training completed
Open doors to customers!

Plan (for 1st milestone)
Create the business plan
Check the plan is accurate and credible

HOW TO BE A SUCCESSFUL GOAL ACHIEVER

Present to Bank Manager
Present to 'other' potential investors
Demonstrate personal funds for project

Tasks (relating specifically to above plan)
Complete rough draft of business plan
Create presentation pack
Ask partner to check it
Organize savings statement
Make appointments with potential investors
Prepare speech for presentation

Now, use the above steps for your own goals. Break each goal down, into the various stages, so you can clearly see what level of detail you need to drill down to.

5

Final Thoughts

"The question isn't who is going to let me; it's who is going to stop me?"
~ Ayn Rand, *The Fountainhead*

The prospect of goal setting may seem daunting at first. However, as we've seen, we all do it, all the time. There are the everyday, seemingly insignificant goals we do by

FINAL THOUGHTS

choice or habit, plus, there are the long term ambitions we dream of, that we're slowly edging toward.

Too often, we make excuses as to why we are not where we want to be, or as close to achieving our dreams as we think we should be. There can be many historical and personal reasons for this. However, with a fresh understanding and clear path for future goal management, your achievements should now be clear-cut, realistic, authentic, and way more exciting. It's time to reset and start afresh.

Throughout the book, we've explored how to:

- Identify what you really want and choose the right goals for *you*
- Avoid self sabotage
- Recognize and control your fears or doubts
- Manage your own expectations
- Effectively set goals, for maximum results
- Identify supportive systems and tools
- Use step by step methods to keep things simple
- Eliminate distractions and overpower obstacles
- Create new, helpful habits
- Be laser focused to turn your goals into a reality
- Become an awesome goal achiever

SECRETS TO GOAL SETTING SUCCESS

When you develop a clear understanding as to *what* goal setting is all about, *why* you need to bother setting them for yourself, and *how* to go about becoming a super-successful goal achiever, your life will move forward at an amazing pace.

Change your actions, change your life!

Hopefully, you will have discovered how simple and highly effective goal setting and goal achievement can really be, especially when you have a positive approach, and genuinely set your mind to it. Goal setting need not be complicated, when you use simple, effective tools, and are passionate about the outcome.

Goals that stimulate your senses and make you feel invigorated when think about the end result, become easily attainable when you combine the right steps toward acheving them.

Well managed goals are guaranteed to deliver results in a faster, easier, and less stressful or confusing manner than poorly thought through goals, which are easily given up on, and are disappointing.

When you know you *can*, and *will* succeed with your goals, you'll feel a powerful new sense of confidence. The past is the past, but is now is now.

FINAL THOUGHTS

Know that when you take the right *actions*, you will get the right *results*.

*"If you have built castles in the air,
your work need not be lost;
that is where they should be.
Now put the foundations under them. "
~ Henry David Thoreau, Walden, 1854*

6

Next Steps

So, with all that said, what should you do next?

We've laid out many different methods, approaches, systems, and steps you can take. The bottom line is, if they work for you, use them. If only certain bits work for you, then only use those bits.

Don't make things too complicated.

NEXT STEPS

Keep things simple. Different goals will require different approaches, depending on their size, timescale, and complexity. Be realistic about the steps you need to take, and the tools that are best suited to support the goal.

For example:

- If you want to drop a dress size before a big event, make sure you set up some helpful, diet oriented daily habits. Note their completion on a chart every day, and stick to them rigidly.

- In your lifetime, you want to run a marathon, but currently don't run. Start off gently, may be aim initially for a small, local charity event, get sponsored, and get going.

- You want to pass your exams, travel round the world, and swim with dolphins. Set up a vision board, identify key milestones, and create some preset rewards for each time you pass a major marker.

- You really want to pay off your mortgage early. Lay out a step by step plan for the financial milestones and tasks you need to focus on. Will you need to take on extra shifts, a second job, or run a small business from home on the weekend? Have you researched the quickest and most effective methods available?

- If you want to build a large brick barbeque in the garden this summer, write out a plan for the materials you'll need, who can help, any tools you'll need to get, instructions required, etc. Break this down into a task list, e.g. print out instructions from the Internet, check brick supplier prices, order bricks, contact Marcus for help, and so forth.

Have you identified which systems, methods or tools are right for you? Have you researched which ones are available, and look good? Or, are you more of a pen and paper person?

Review specific chapters or sections in this book. Reconsider the content, and how it applies to you, in more depth. Focus clearly on using steps that work for you, master the relevant skills and you'll benefit by feeling more confident, uplifted, energized, determined and ready to take on the world.

Complete the exercises in the previous section. Use the PDF links in the Worksheet section. Print them out or

NEXT STEPS

create your own personalized template. Use them to work through your thought processes, and/or record any steps you need to make.

Read more, research more. Take time to learn more about the art of goal achievement. Dig further into areas you still feel unsure of, or want to delve into, in more depth. See our recommended reading list below, for further reading suggestions.

Stop over-planning, and start doing. Get cracking, and make some great stuff happen!

"There are two things to aim at in life; first to get what you want, and after that to enjoy it. Only the wisest of mankind has achieved the second."
~ Logan Pearsall Smith

There are no magical methods to setting a goal and having the results miraculously appear. Whatever it is you want, especially if it's worthwhile, will take time and effort. However, the actual goal setting in itself can be kept simple.

Goal achievements meanwhile, require vision, focus, and commitment.

You are as capable as the next person. If you want to see your dreams become a reality, you need to take meaningful action, be consistent, stay focused and passionate about the results, and you *will* be successful.

Make a promise to yourself that you will be a goal achiever, and resolve to make it happen.

"The vision must be followed by the venture.
It is not enough to stare up the steps
- we must step up the stairs."
~ Vance Havner

Further recommended reading - If you would like to learn more about successful goal achievement you may also enjoy the following titles by other authors:

The 7 Habits of Highly Effective People – Stephen R. Covey

Goals!: How to Get Everything You Want -- Faster Than You Ever Thought Possible – Brian Tracy

Manage Your Day-To-Day: Build Your Routine, Find Your Focus, and Sharpen Your Creative Mind – Jocelyn K. Glei

Mind Mapping For Dummies – Florian Rustler

NEXT STEPS

Mini Habits: Smaller Habits, Bigger Results – Stephen Guise

Fear: Essential Wisdom For Getting Through The Storm – Thich Nhat Hanh

Getting Things Done: How to achieve stress-free productivity – Dave Allen

*We also have other **FeelFabToday Guides** available, which you may enjoy:*

www.feelfabtoday.com

When you learn, and then practice, the art of effective goal setting, you can begin to create rapid and lasting changes in your life. Be clear on your true goals and ignite your passion; you'll soon discover how simple it is to create a life of happiness and success.

7

About The Author

Rachel Robins is the creator behind the *feelfabtoday* products. She has a passion for exploring and sharing ideas that centre on positivity & self improvement.

Rachel focuses her attention on how to help others feel as good as possible - using realistic feel-good techniques, healthy tips & a hefty dose of positivity. At the heart of the *feelfabtoday* products are methods on how to feel fabulous, look great, achieve more & live positively. These products are created with the help of a small team of talented people, who add their wisdom, knowledge and skills to the process, and who Rachel would like to thank for their continued efforts and support.

Rachel has worked in various senior management roles, where she's successfully practiced the art of conflict management, leadership, negotiation and change management, plus she's trained many teams and individuals to achieve successful, target driven outcomes. Her range of interpersonal skills, life experience and self-help knowledge means she's able to

ABOUT THE AUTHOR

share practical steps on how to take control of your life, develop a positive self image, and feel good about yourself.

She's put together this FeelFabToday Guide on *Secrets To Goal Setting Success*, so others can discover how to achieve what they really want, using simple and manageable steps. Rachel's also written additional FeelFabToday Guides, designed to explore different areas of self empowerment, confidence building and feeling good about yourself.

8

And Finally

We really hope you found this book helpful.

We'd love it if you'd also join us at:
twitter.com/feelfabtoday
www.feelfabtoday.com

Many thanks for reading our book -
we wish you every success in achieving
everything you *really want* in life…

Printed in Poland
by Amazon Fulfillment
Poland Sp. z o.o., Wrocław